SOTHEBY PARKE BERNET'S LUXURY PROPERTIES

Sotheby Parke Bernet International Realty Corporation®

A WALLABY BOOK

PUBLISHED BY POCKET BOOKS NEW YORK

Sotheby Parke Bernet International Realty®

Charles H. Seilheimer, Jr.
President

Edward Lee Cave
Chairman

corporate headquarters:
980 Madison Avenue, New York 10021
tel. (212) 472-3465
telex: 232643

Northeast
Clark P. Halstead, Jr., Vice President
980 Madison Avenue, New York 10021
tel. (212) 472-3465

Southeast
Rodney J. Dillard, Vice President
155 Worth Avenue, Palm Beach, Florida 33480
tel. (305) 659-3555

Mid-Atlantic
41 Culpeper Street, Warrenton, Virginia 22186
tel. (703) 347-7577
Washington—tel. (202) 273-1136

New England
George C. Ballantyne, Regional Manager
980 Madison Avenue, New York 10021
tel. (212) 472-3465

West Coast
Hall F. Willkie, Regional Manager
7660 Beverly Boulevard, Los Angeles, California 90036
tel. (213) 937-5130

Sotheby Parke Bernet's Luxury Properties

Compiled and edited by:
Shelly Nohowel, *Marketing Director*

Contents

Letter of Introduction

We at Sotheby Parke Bernet International Realty Corporation are proud to present our first annual volume, a selection of properties which have either been sold or are currently being offered for sale by our firm.

Over a period of two centuries, Sotheby's has earned a reputation as the foremost worldwide marketplace for buyers and sellers of fine art property. With our established international clientele, proven expertise in global marketing, and resources which include a network of 36 offices throughout the world, it was a logical extension of Sotheby's activities and experience to serve also as a marketplace for buyers and sellers of luxury residential, estate and farm properties. In the three years since its founding, Sotheby Parke Bernet International Realty has become an international leader in the sale of prestigious real estate through negotiated brokerage.

We are often asked what criteria our firm uses in selecting the properties we market. Rather than price, the major factor is a unique or distinguishing feature which places the property above the limitations of the local market. Achieving maximum value for a distinctive property requires an organization capable of exposing it in the more lucrative, national and international sales arena. We at Sotheby's are in a unique position to assist an ever-growing worldwide clientele; our public relations and direct mail specialists, in-house advertising agency and proven sales teams are all professionals seasoned in the complexities of finding a meeting ground for select buyers and sellers of fine property. In addition, our firm recognizes the vital importance of the local real estate broker, both in the listing and selling of property, and cooperates with the most qualified representative in each community where we offer properties for sale.

The extraordinary properties in these pages offer a wide variety of architecture and setting, but they share the elegance of lifestyle and level of quality increasingly sought by Sotheby's international clientele. In a true sense, these properties are "works of art" and we are pleased to have this opportunity to share them with you.

Charles H. Seilheimer, Jr.
PRESIDENT

Edward Lee Cave
CHAIRMAN

New England

The past lives in the cities and villages of old New England—a proud sense of history and mature tradition unlike that of any other region in the nation. It is a past reflected in the celebrated architecture of the New England states: from the 1820's "Richmond House" on historic Elm Street in Woodstock, Vermont, to the elegant early 19th century "Proctor House" on Boston Commons. This superb architectural heritage continues into the present, with such properties as the dramatic hilltop contemporary on Martha's Vineyard, winner of the 1975 American Institute of Architects award for vacation homes. All of these properties are represented by Sotheby Parke Bernet Realty, now a major presence in the marketing of fine New England property.

The area encompassing Vermont, New Hampshire, Rhode Island, Massachusetts and Maine is a region of extraordinary natural beauty, with mountains and hills, luxuriant forests, famed ski resorts at places like Stowe and Killington, and marvelous sailing and boating along a rocky, largely unspoiled coastline. From the broad teakwood decks of "Saheda," a vacation retreat nestled among the rocks in the prestigious summer colony of Seal Harbor, Maine, one may watch the lobster boats and yacht races during the summer months. Undeveloped oceanfront properties like Maine's Cape Rosier or the Nova Scotian hunting retreat called, quite appropriately, "Shangri-La," answer a deep-felt need for unspoiled wilderness—yet another New England tradition.

Sotheby Parke Bernet is also offering fine New England farms like Elm Hill, near Clarendon, Vermont, and residential estates like Wheelbarrow Hill, near the Tanglewood Music festival in Stockbridge, Massachusetts, and "Chailey" in Newburyport, near the New Hampshire border, Sotheby's first combined art and real estate sale in New England. Some of the most substantial sales in New England residential real estate have been handled by the firm, with established local brokers complementing Sotheby's marketing expertise. Vaucluse Farm, a magnificent 230-acre waterfront estate just outside Newport, received what is believed to be a record price for a residential property in that area. Still, New England has some of the most attractive land values in America; property that is most certain to appreciate in the years to come.

Sotheby Parke Bernet Realty is today at the forefront of a major resurgence of interest in the grand New England summer home. This 19th century phenomenon is on the rise as the nation's concern for energy conservation makes the permanent vacation retreat more and more attractive. The firm is offering for sale the shore-hugging summer home of the late Nelson Rockefeller in Seal Harbor; a rambling 75-year-old beach house in the quiet summer colony of Watch Hill, Rhode Island; and in picturesque Wilton Center, New Hampshire, a beautifully restored 19th century Federal-style residence on 15 wooded acres. The most famous of all America's summer colonies is, of course, Newport, Rhode Island, home of the renown summer yacht races and tennis week. Here, the firm recently sold Hammersmith Farm, the Newport White House of President John F. Kennedy and former residence of Mrs. Hugh Auchincloss, to an enterprising attorney who has converted it into a Kennedy and Newport museum. And, on the old whaling island of Nantucket, an 11-acre estate with a spacious Cape Cod-style residence recently fetched a record price for a summer home there.

THE RICHMOND HOUSE Woodstock, Vermont

One of the "Elm Street Houses", a group of 19th Century residences located in this picturesque Vermont town, this stately 1820's Federal residence stands adjacent to the First Congregational Church of 1889 and is listed in Dana's *History Of Woodstock*. Two beautifully maintained acres with large pines, maples and elms surround the rose brick house with its finely carved Adam mantels and random-width floors. Terraced lawns slope down to frontage on the Ottauquechee River with splendid views of the surrounding hills. This charming New England setting is located just 2½ hours from Boston and twenty minutes from superb winter sports at Killington.

THE YELLOW HOUSE Wilton Center, New Hampshire

In the heart of picturesque Wilton Center, this charming 180-year-old estate is as perfect a slice of old New England as one could ever find, while offering all modern conveniences for year-round family living. The 6-bedroom Federal-style residence affords beautiful vistas of the property's 15 acres of rolling lawns and pine woodland, and the interiors have been meticulously maintained with attention paid to the original features of the home: wideboard floors, fine paneling, small paned windows and 4 brick fireplaces throughout.

DIONIS BEACH ESTATE Nantucket, Massachusetts

This beautiful 11-acre beachfront vacation estate with generously proportioned, modified Cape Cod-style residence justly sold for the highest price ever for a summer residence on Nantucket. This historic island, renowned for its carefully preserved communities dating from the 18th Century, has long been a favorite destination for vacationers and connoisseurs of American architecture.

ELM HILL FARM Clarendon, Vermont

One of the larger farms in Vermont, this 575-acre property has been owned by the same family since the late 18th Century. Presently run as a small dairying operation with separate caretaker's house and guest cottage, the pastoral setting represents a fine opportunity for the gentleman farmer as well as for the investor.

OCEANFRONT SUMMER RESIDENCE
Watch Hill, Rhode Island

In the charming oceanfront colony of Watch Hill, noted for its air of quiet and privacy, this early 1900's residence, with its broad lawns stretching to 360 feet of private Atlantic beachfront, is the ideal place for a traditional New England beach summer.

OCEANFRONT DEVELOPMENT
Cape Rosier, Maine (*bottom*)

This extraordinary 412-acre property with 2½ miles of shoreline represents a rare opportunity to own one of the most extensive oceanfront parcels on the Atlantic Seaboard.

THE PROCTOR HOUSE
Boston, Massachusetts (*opposite*)

The elegance of early 19th Century Boston pervades this architecturally important residence facing the charming Public Garden of the Boston Common. This lovely townhouse built in the Greek Revival Style is situated on Beacon Hill, an enchanting neighborhood of historic townhouses and quaint streets.

"CHAILEY" Newburyport, Massachusetts

The site of Sotheby Parke Bernet's first combined art and real estate sale in New England, this charming estate was sold on the same day that the on-premises auction was held. Noted for its prize-winning gardens and lovely setting on the Merrimack River, "Chailey" dates from the 18th Century, with later additions by architect William Perry of Colonial Williamsburg.

HAMMERSMITH FARM Newport, Rhode Island

Formerly the home of Mrs. Hugh D. Auchincloss, mother of Jacqueline Kennedy Onassis, and the last farm in America's most popular "watering spot", Hammersmith was also the Newport White House of the late President John F. Kennedy. A lovely 55-acre property with one of Newport's grandest summer cottages, this estate was purchased by an imaginative lawyer who has opened it to the public as a Kennedy and Newport museum.

THE ANCHORAGE Seal Harbor, Maine

Formerly the summer home of the late Vice President Nelson A. Rockefeller, this property is located at the tip of its own four-acre peninsula in one of New England's most prestigious summer colonies. The house was carefully conceived by Nelson Rockefeller himself to follow the curve of the shore and the contour of the land, fitting unobtrusively into the landscape and providing spectacular views from every major room. Surrounding the house are naturally landscaped grounds which complement the rugged coastline. A heated saltwater swimming pool nestles among the rocks.

SHANGRI-LA Yarmouth, Nova Scotia, Canada

Unique on the North American continent, this extraordinary estate encompasses nearly 600 acres of unspoiled wilderness and seven miles of ocean frontage on Nova Scotia's picturesque coast. A sportsman's dream, Shangri-La is presently used as a private wild boar hunting preserve which is self-supporting, providing both revenue and recreation.

"SAHEDA" Seal Harbor, Maine

Located in Seal Harbor on Maine's Mt. Desert Island, this contemporary residence is spectacularly designed for its dramatic natural setting overlooking the rocky coastline 60 feet below. Its expansive teakwood deck overlooks the sea, where lobster boats journey year-round and sail boats from the nearby yacht clubs race during the summer months. Built with only the finest materials and superb craftsmanship, the residence features radiant heating in every room, a private well, and an electric generator, permitting year-round occupancy.

PROSPECT FARM
Sherborn, Massachusetts

Tastefully converted from an old barn in the manor of an English
country house, this well-designed residence on 38 acres in one of
Boston's most desirable western suburbs skillfully combines old
New England charm with all modern conveniences.

WHEELBARROW HILL Great Barrington, Massachusetts

Less than a 2½-hour drive from either New York or Boston, this 300-acre hilltop estate is near the renowned Tanglewood Music Festival and Stockbridge Summer Theatre. In an area of distinguished homes, the estate boasts its own stable with paddock, two guest houses, including a striking contemporary poolhouse, and grounds teeming with deer and pheasant.

VAUCLUSE FARM Portsmouth, Rhode Island

Farmland, meadow, gardens, and of course, the sea are the backdrop for this splendid Georgian mansion and its 230 waterfront acres. Situated just outside Newport, and known for its prize-winning Jersey cattle, this important property realized a sale in excess of two million dollars, believed to be the most substantial purchase price on record for a New England residence.

ROCKLAND FARM
South Dartmouth, Massachusetts (*opposite*)

Located in an area of exclusive waterfront homes, this unique contemporary house is extremely private yet easily accessible by car, plane or boat. From its indoor pool beneath a 30-foot beamed cathedral ceiling are beautiful views of the Elizabeth Islands to the southeast and Martha's Vineyard beyond. Ideal for entertaining, this estate has its own beach, tennis court, bridle paths, and 100-year-old bowling alley with original pins and balls.

MARTHA'S VINEYARD CONTEMPORARY
Chilmark, Massachusetts

Winner of the 1975 American Institute of Architecture award for vacation homes, this distinctive contemporary residence is privately situated atop the highest hill on Martha's Vineyard, one of the best loved vacation spots in the Northeast. The unusual home, specially designed to accommodate the seaside environment, affords magnificent views of the surrounding area in three directions.

Northeast

New York, New Jersey and Connecticut boast many fine, even prototypical residential communities, estates, summer colonies and farms, drawing their vitality at least in part from their closeness to the greater New York area. Yet this is extraordinary country in its own right, with beautifully maintained lawns, verdant woods and fields, rivers and waterways, an almost European climate and a diversity of luxury properties in what has traditionally been the area with the largest concentration of wealth and population in the United States.

Among the premiere residential communities is Greenwich and its environs in Fairfield County, Connecticut, which have experienced an upsurge in real estate value because of reasonable taxes and an attractive, countrified location easily accessible to New York City. Here, Sotheby Parke Bernet Realty sold the imposing 46-acre Reynwood Estate for well over a million dollars. Just south of Fairfield County is Westchester County in New York State, where Sotheby's, in conjunction with the Houlihan Company, sold the 40-acre Sugarhill Farm for over $750,000. And on Long Island's North Shore, home to the legendary families of New York finance, the firm completed a sale in 1977 of a contemporary residence on Cooper's Bluff for the highest price achieved in Nassau County that year.

In suburban New Jersey, exclusive residential properties are generally located in and around Far Hills, Rumson, Alpine and in Princeton, where the firm is offering "Landfall," a magnificent Tudor mansion built for Robert Roebling, son of the Brooklyn Bridge designer. "Rio Vista," a 300-acre land parcel in Alpine and Cresskill and the largest unimproved residential development property in the immediate environs of Manhattan, was recently sold for over six million dollars.

The firm has also made substantial sales in many of the affluent country and resort areas in the tri-state region, including Fishers Island, the Hamptons, the Berkshire foothills, the Millbrook area and the Hudson River estates in Dutchess and Litchfield Counties. Our story of Fishers Island is a very special one. In this elite summer colony established generations ago by the most conservative of our nation's "old guard" and still home to the families of Pittsburgh Steel, Dupont and Weyerhaeuser, Sotheby's sensitive marketing efforts resulted in the sale of six major properties within the past year. While this "new blood," who appreciate and will maintain the special quality of Fishers, include purchasers such as a lawyer from Cleveland, a Parisian oil heir and a Hollywood film producer, the most notable transaction was that of Medieval Seaside Castle, purchased by an international financier with a London-based business. The "castle," formerly owned by Simmons mattress heir Sanford Simmons, was purchased for nearly twice the price of any other property ever sold on the island.

CROW'S NEST Fishers Island, New York

Nestled in the crest of a hill on one of the highest points of the island, this imposing residence offers panoramic sights of the Connecticut shoreline and the North Fork of Long Island, with one of the choicest views from the extraordinary great hall, a huge ship-like room with beamed cathedral ceiling and eight-foot-wide stone fireplace.

MEDIEVAL SEASIDE CASTLE
East Point, Fishers Island, New York

Reminiscent of a Norman Medieval keep, this Brittany-style manor house is a Gothic fantasy of gables, turrets, and great halls of granite and oak. From its dramatic setting on 6½ acres of boulder-strewn oceanfront, the keep is a yachtsman's landmark with spectacular views sweeping over the sea in three directions. Truly the castle is one of the most unusual vacation homes in the East.

QUAKER HILL STOCK FARM

Pawling, New York

This fine late 19th-century Colonial is situated on 280 acres of pasture, cropland and forest with beautiful westerly views of the Hudson Valley. The immaculately maintained farm, just 65 miles from Manhattan, was recently used for the breeding of Morgan horses and a prize-winning dairy herd. The residence is complemented by a greenhouse and artist's studio, a pool house and manager's cottage, in addition to several professionally equipped farm buildings.

AKNUSTI ESTATE Delaware County, New York

In light of the outstanding thoroughbred breeding incentives in-troduced in New York state two years ago, this 1800-acre horse and game farm—one of the largest farm complexes in New York—presents a very attractive investment opportunity to the serious horse breeder. In the western foothills of the Catskills, three hours from New York City, the property features a gracious nine-bedroom estate house plus seven staff houses, a large stable complex with indoor track and a complete game farm with one-acre duck pond and kennels.

BONNIE BRAE FARM Millbrook, New York

With numerous working farms and handsome residences of country gentry, the Millbrook area of Dutchess County, home of the world-famous Millbrook Fox Hunt, has preserved a gracious New England ambiance in a splendid setting of densely wooded hills and rolling pastures. The 170-acre "Bonnie Brae," with its extensive riding facilities, private pond stocked with bass, and pristine white frame colonial residence, provides a distinguished refuge within weekend commuting range of New York City.

CLOVE CREEK FARM Poughquag, New York

Located in the town of Poughquag, an Indian word meaning "lovely stream," this productive farm-estate of 535 contiguous acres includes an historic main residence built in 1812.

Presently owned by Franklin D. Roosevelt, Jr., the farm is well suited to either cultivation or cattle and horse raising, and provides an ideal location for the agrarian or potential country dweller.

VALLEY CASTLE Cornwall, Connecticut

Standing in its own private valley on 250 acres with a pond, stream and waterfall, this dramatic stone manor offers an impressive picture of Medieval splendor. Wood beamed ceilings, tall fireplaces, stone pillars and massive archways all contribute to the romance of the estate, with complete renovations in the main residence and numerous stone guest dwellings allowing for the comforts of modern living.

QUARRY LAKE
Northcastle, New York (*opposite*)

Rare cobalt blue waters and a white sand beach at the bottom of a 70-foot chasm is the breathtaking focus of this 45-acre mid-Westchester property. Ideal for either a year-round family residence or an attractive corporate retreat within one hour of Manhattan, the wooded estate boasts a large Georgian Colonial residence, beach house, tennis court and stable building.

33

HOBBY BARN Pound Ridge, New York

A charming converted barn dating back to 1780 is the focus of this 7-acre wooded setting with English-style border gardens and a pond frequented by deer. Stone fireplaces, natural barn siding and carved pine doors contribute to the rustic elegance of this magical country house, featured on several occasions in *House and Garden*.

NEW POND Carmel, New York

This Scandanavian-inspired contemporary residence overlooks its own nine-acre spring-fed pond on an 89-acre site of hills and woodlands. The secluded country estate is only 80 minutes by car from mid-Manhattan, and within easy reach of urban centers in Westchester and Connecticut.

"SEASCAPE" Rumson, New Jersey

For amplitude of space and beauty of setting, very few estates in the New York area can match this property. Standing well secluded on its ample grounds and surrounding woods on one of the coastlines highest promontories, and close to the famed resorts of the Jersey shore, this fine Georgian residence and full complement of outbuildings offers the best of country living without sacrificing proximity to New York City.

THE HARKNESS ESTATE
Snedens Landing, New York *(opposite)*

This splendid 7½-acre estate is in a heavily wooded area on the Palisades overlooking the Hudson River, with a lively history dating back to the 18th Century. The residence was built in the 1950's for Katharine Cornell and greatly enlarged in 1967 by the dance patron Rebekah Harkness. Today, the estate complete with its own magnificent dance studio, is the new country home of one of America's leading Motown singers.

COOPER'S BLUFF CONTEMPORARY
Cove Neck, Long Island, New York

Dappled with dogwood and azalea gardens and bordered by 1,200 feet of beach on Oyster Bay Harbor, this striking Cove Neck residence boasts a 180-degree view from its magnificent site 130 feet above the bay. The multi-level home, reminiscent of Frank Lloyd Wright's "prairie school" designs, takes full advantage of the glorious surroundings through the generous use of glass, skylights and terraces: nature provides this residence with its most spectacular furnishings.

TIRRANNA New Canaan, Connecticut

"Tirranna" is an Australian aboriginal word meaning "running water." It is also the name given to this 1955 Frank Lloyd Wright residence, already considered a part of America's architectural heritage. Located in a 13-acre botanical park in one of New York City's finest outlying suburban areas, the long, single-level residence overlooks a lower semi-circular deck and pool area with two ponds, a spillway, and a 100-foot fountain jet below. To create these ponds, Wright and Frank Okamura, designer of the Brooklyn Botanical Gardens, widened and deepened the Noroton River to flow through the property; and the renowned landscape architect Charles Middeleer designed and executed the gardens, where rare specimen plantings flourish amid an older growth of oak and beech trees. The interior of the house incorporates design features of Wright's peerless mastery, including Phillipine mahogany ceilings, floors and woodwork, as well as Wright's fabric designs, carpet layouts, and original furniture, some designed especially for "Tirranna."

REYNWOOD Greenwich, Connecticut

Within the seclusion of 45 rolling, pine-wooded acres in the prestigious back country of Greenwich, this baronial estate has a storybook setting which speaks quietly of Old World traditions rarely found so near a major metropolitan area. Inside the Gothic-style manor house, the spirit of Medieval times is warmly recreated with pine paneling, pegged hardwood floors, and architectural moldings that complement the stone walls and vaulted cathedral ceilings. The recent sale of "Reynwood" was one of the most substantial real estate transactions in Connecticut.

LORD'S COVE RETREAT Old Lyme, Connecticut

With views over the water to Old Saybrook and Essex, this heavily wooded 25-acre estate borders on 1,000 feet of the Connecticut near where the river meets the sea. The comfortable main residence, guest cottage, greenhouse and boathouse on the property insure a gracious country life near some of Connecticut's most picturesque and historic coastal villages.

"LOCHMERE" Little Silver, New Jersey

With its location in New Jersey's most luxurious seaside residential area and a 1,400-foot waterfrontage on the South Shrewsbury River, this is an ideal estate for the outdoor enthusiast. The lovely property features a distinctive traditional residence set in beautifully landscaped grounds, and affords pleasing views over the river to the Atlantic dunes beyond.

SPECTACULAR CONTEMPORARY RESIDENCE
Alpine, New Jersey

This extraordinary contemporary residence, designed by architect Norman Jaffe and completed three years ago at a cost of over $2,300,000, incorporates some of the most advanced aspects of modern architecture. Exterior walls constructed mostly of glass and stone take full advantage of the natural surroundings and panoramic views from the marvelous location on the Palisades. Built in three wings—the entertainment wing, the recreation wing, and the family wing—with such distinctive features as an indoor pool and greenhouse/atrium, a motorized movie screen, and a see-through fireplace, this house has been featured on the cover of *Interior Design* magazine. Situated in an exclusive residential area less than ten miles from Manhattan amid six park-like acres, surrounded by dense woods with no other residences in sight, this architectural triumph has mastered its sense of spaciousness, comfort and style.

47

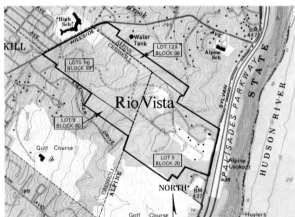

"RIO VISTA" Alpine and Cresskill, New Jersey

The summer farm-estate of a prominent international family during the early 1900's, "Rio Vista's" 300 wooded acres, located just five miles north of the George Washington Bridge, represent the largest undeveloped luxury residential development parcel in the New York region. Reminiscent of days when grand estates lined the edge of the cliffs along the Hudson, the Tiffany-designed stone chapel and the Gothic clock tower, now a regional landmark, are among the remaining structures on the Palisades property.

Manhattan

In Manhattan, real estate prices have risen nearly ninety percent since 1977, a remarkable surge of interest and commitment reflecting the general renaissance of New York City life in the late Seventies. With a fiscal situation vastly improved since the near bankruptcy of several years ago, as well as cultural advantages offered by no other city in the world, New York City—and Manhattan in particular—has entered a period in which fine properties are in high demand and relatively short supply. Apartments and townhouses on the East Side are selling faster than ever before, and a Fifth Avenue address is once again the most prestigious address on earth.

The presence of large numbers of foreign buyers on the Manhattan real estate market should be no surprise: New York City is widely considered a safe and reliable investment in a politically secure country with a relatively stable currency. And clearly, no other city in the world can offer the cultural enticements of New York. The art museums house among the most impressive collections in the world; symphony, ballet and theatrical performances are available for both classical and contemporary audiences; and trend-setters from around the globe continue to find here the leaders of fashion and design.

But affluent Americans have also taken active roles in New York's real estate boom, moving from the country and the suburbs to participate in Manhattan's rich, almost inexhaustible lifestyle. As a big city, New York can offer a special kind of privacy and anonymity, which Sotheby Parke Bernet Realty promotes with its discreet, professional services. The following sales illustrate the background and diversity of our clients: Henry J. Heinz II's spectacular Sutton Place triplex apartment overlooking the East River was purchased by a client from Pittsburgh. A townhouse on East 65th Street was bought by a prominent Broadway producer. Kenneth Jay Lane's townhouse on East 38th Street is now Liza Minnelli's first "home of her own." An elegant 18-room apartment at the prestigious 820 Fifth Avenue was recently bought by a European, another apartment in the same building by a South American. A duplex at 950 Fifth Avenue is now owned by a Venezuelan client and a nine-room apartment in the Hotel Pierre on Fifth Avenue by a prominent Latin American.

Unlike the rest of the country, where Sotheby Parke Bernet handles property on an exclusive listing basis, Manhattan properties can be listed on a non-exclusive basis for a six percent commission. More important properties, however, are designated exclusive listings and given worldwide professional marketing, and a ten percent commission is charged.

820 FIFTH AVENUE New York City

This splendid cooperative residence, with its prestigious address and treetop-level views across Central Park, typifies all the best in Manhattan living. Few apartments of such noble proportions and magnificence of detail and decoration can boast the surprising intimacy so skillfully created here by Jansen, Inc. for its art-collecting owners.

CONTEMPORARY MAISONETTE New York City

Internationally renowned interior designer Valerian Rybar planned this glamorous Sutton Place apartment as his personal New York residence. Located in one of Manhattan's most exclusive areas, the sumptuously designed ground-level maisonette incorporates many unique design elements, including stainless steel flooring and the extensive use of mirrors, chrome, tortoiseshell and luxurious fabrics.

MURRAY HILL TOWNHOUSE New York City

Formerly the East Side residence of jewelry designer Kenneth Jay Lane, this charming house in Manhattan's historic Murray Hill section has been purchased by entertainer and Broadway performer Liza Minnelli as her first "home of her own." Mr. Lane's eclectic art collection was auctioned at record prices by Sotheby Parke Bernet just prior to the real estate sale.

CONTEMPORARY COLLECTOR'S RESIDENCE
New York City

In 1975, architect Keith Kroeger and interior designer Filippa Naess collaborated on a clean contemporary design within the proportions of one of Manhattan's grand older buildings. Beginning with handsome, spacious rooms and the Moorish arches and columns of a 1920-era apartment, the sleek new design washes the uncluttered, flowing interiors in natural sunlight, making this an ideal residence for an art collector.

JACOBEAN DUPLEX New York City

Architectural elements taken from a late 19th century New-port residence have helped create a baronial European ambiance in this most remarkable Manhattan apartment. The commanding double-height living room/library is fitted with oak bookcases and boasts a large stone fireplace with carved over-mantle. The gourmet kitchen and pantry, which combine Old World charm with the modern conveniences necessary for sophisticated entertainment, surely delighted the apartment's new owner, a world renowned restauranteur.

STATELY APARTMENT RESIDENCE New York City

On East 72nd Street, between Fifth and Madison Avenues, this full-floor cooperative apartment residence is located in what is often cited as one of New York's ten best buildings. Renovations by French & Company include exquisite marble floors, gilded hardware throughout, handpainted French wallpapers and elegant 18th Century boiseries.

PALAZZO TRIPLEX New York City

The former Manhattan residence of the Henry J. Heinz II
family, and Claire Booth Luce before them, this magnificent apartment is truly reminiscent of a Venetian
palace. An elegant 21-room triplex, the apartment offers
breathtaking views in three directions of the East River
and beyond. The lavish ambiance of this luxurious residence epitomizes the best of Manhattan. Here too,
Sotheby Parke Bernet coordinated the sale of a most outstanding art collection.

SUTTON PLACE RESIDENCE New York City

Boasting the architectural detail and dignity of London's Mayfair, this 13-room apartment on Sutton Place affords a spectacular view from its prestigious location overlooking the East River and the building's charming private river gardens.

PHILIP JOHNSON TOWNHOUSE New York City

The only Philip Johnson-designed townhouse in New York City was completely reconstructed from an 1860's carriage house. The celebrated architect blended oriental and modernist inspiration in a brilliant simple design of glass and garden, creating a place of refuge and beauty in an unrivaled location in midtown. Originally built as an in-town retreat for Mrs. John D. Rockefeller III, it could also serve ideally as a corporate guest house or private gallery.

Mid-Atlantic

The Mid-Atlantic region has firm roots in the history of America. It is one of the first areas of the country to be settled, famed for its beautiful countryside and gracious homes as well as for its elegant sporting traditions. The market for luxury residential real estate in Delaware, Pennsylvania, Maryland and Virginia has been strong and will continue on its decidedly upward tend.

Most of these properties are rural estates with working farms or equestrian facilities: fox hunting, steeplechasing, polo, racing and breeding are significant attractions of the Mid-Atlantic states. Properties in Virginia, in particular, with unspoiled countryside in the center of the eastern seaboard are selling at a faster pace than new listings can be obtained. Foreign buyers, mostly from Europe, comprise about half this booming market, and, according to William T. Stevens, a prominent Virginia realtor and Sotheby affiliate, to the European, real estate is a sanctuary for the individual as well as for his capital. Also of interest are the sporting estates of both the Maryland and Virginia Eastern Shore, where sailing, waterfowl shooting, oystering and crabbing are a way of life. The plantation homes and historic properties of Maryland and northern Virginia, many of them two to three hundred years old, have the additional advantage of proximity to the nation's capital, and attract a wide range of individuals of all ages and professions, from business executives to retired persons who enjoy the change of seasons and seek a warm, but not a tropical, climate.

In the Mid-Atlantic region, Sotheby Parke Bernet Realty has represented such glorious properties as Corbin Hall, a 470-acre estate on Virginia's Eastern Shore with a faithfully restored 18th century mansion—a National Register Landmark—recently purchased for a record price by an upstate New Yorker; "Little England," an historic 62-acre estate in Virginia's Gloucester County, with a plantation house dating from the early 18th century; "Nanzatico" in King George County, next to Mt. Vernon, the finest 18th century frame mansion in Virginia; and Belfield, an estate in the Shenandoah Valley known far and wide for its award-winning gardens.

For all their magnificence, these properties are both productive and livable places: Virginia and Maryland have been havens for horse enthusiasts since the first European landed gentry settled in this country hundreds of years ago. Among the fabulous equestrian properties Sotheby Parke Bernet has offered for sale are "The Meadow," a 2,652-acre breeding farm near Doswell, Virginia, where Triple Crown winner Secretariat was born and trained, recently sold for over $2,500,000; "Blenheim," the 257-acre Charlottesville retreat owned by William Hammerstein, grandson of famed lyricist Oscar Hammerstein II; "Beauregard," one of the largest viable farms suitable for breeding operations in Virginia's legendary hunt country. In Maryland, "Tacaro," a well-known breeding farm with 388 acres on the Chesapeake Bay, and Edgehill Farm, a short distance from Laurel, Bowie and Pimlico Raceways, are both extremely attractive equestrian properties.

COUNTRY ESTATE Greenville, Delaware

This fine residence is located only 3 miles from Wilmington in the heart of Delaware's famed estate country. Complete with stable and pool, the property is typical of the sophisticated informality of the region.

GEORGIAN ESTATE Centerville, Delaware

This superbly proportioned and maintained Georgian mansion surveys over 40 acres of meadow and woods from its private hilltop location, several miles from the heart of Wilmington.

"TACARO" Tracy's Landing, Maryland

This well-proportioned brick mansion built in 1938 commands impressive views over 388 acres to the Chesapeake Bay, yet is only 35 minutes from the nation's capital. Well known as a horse breeding farm, "Tacaro" sports brick stables, silos and cattle barns, a testament to the quality of construction and care of maintenance.

"MELFIELD"
Eastern Shore, Maryland (*opposite*)

A 183-acre estate near Centerville and the junction of the Chester and Corsica Rivers on Maryland's lovely Eastern Shore, "Melfield" boasts a completely renovated Colonial brick mansion that is unusually successful at blending modern comfort and charm.

EDGEHILL FARM
Glyndon, Maryland (*opposite below*)

The choice location, manageable dimensions and expert facilities of Edgehill make this one of Maryland hunt country's most desireable farms. Adjacent to Alfred G. Vanderbilt's Sagamore Farm and a short distance from Laurel, Bowie and Pimlico Raceways, the property's 87 acres, with full complement of barn and stable buildings, attract both the expert breeder and the weekend equestrian, while the charming limestone residence encourages hospitable country living just 30 minutes from Baltimore.

"BELFIELD" Lexington, Virginia

A skillful blending of Norman, Tudor and Elizabethan-style architecture in an award-winning garden setting has made "Belfield" one of the best known estates in the historic Shenandoah Valley. Designed by famed Virginia landscape architect Charles Gillette, the splendid gardens have for decades been a regular stop of touring horticulturists during Historic Garden Week in Virginia.

"LITTLE ENGLAND" Gloucester County, Virginia

Located at the tip of its own peninsula on the York River directly across from the site of Cornwallis' surrender to General Washington, this National and Virginia Register property boasts one of the finest and most meticulously maintained manor houses in Virginia. A daffodil farm in former years, the 62-acre estate has for decades beckoned horticultural enthusiasts and architectural historians alike.

"BLENHEIM" Charlottesville, Virginia

Situated on 257 acres, with views to the rolling foothills of the Shenandoah Mountains beyond, this farm with separate "atheneum" and numerous outbuildings is a perfect retreat for the sportsman or the seeker of inspiration and solitude.

"EDNAM" Albemarle County, Virginia

One of the finest development opportunities in the mid-Atlantic, this superb 35-acre property adjoins both the famed Farmington Country Club and the Boars Head Inn and Sports Complex near Charlottesville, Virginia. Minutes from the University and complete with late Victorian mansion, this estate could also be adapted to institutional use.

CORBIN HALL Accomack County, Virginia

A Virginia and National Register Landmark, Corbin Hall is revered as one of the architectural masterpieces of Virginia's famed Eastern Shore, where the lifestyle has changed little in the past century. The 18th-Century mansion, basically unaltered, commands views over the 470-acre property to fabled Chincoteague Island across the Bay. The owner's superb collection of English antiques and furnishings were sold in an on-premises sale by Sotheby Parke Bernet.

THE MEADOW Doswell, Caroline County, Virginia

One of the finest Thoroughbred farms in America, The Meadow is known as the home of Triple Crown winner Secretariat, Riva Ridge and other outstanding champions of the turf. The farm of over 2,600 acres features indoor and outdoor training tracks, stabling for over 200 horses and additional farm dependencies which compliment the colonial manor house.

"NANZATICO" King George County, Virginia

"Nanzatico," described as probably the most formal frame 18th-Century mansion in Virginia next to Mt. Vernon, is listed on the Virginia and National Landmarks Register. Set on over 70 acres of fertile land and commanding 2,000 feet of frontage on the Rappahanock River, this manor house is located close to Washington, D.C. in the "northern neck" of Virginia, a haven for the waterfowl sportsman.

EYREVILLE Cheriton, Eastern Shore, Virginia

Surrounded on 3 sides by tributaries of the Chesapeake Bay, the 1,000-acre Eyreville deserves its reputation as one of the finest and most productive farms on Virginia's Eastern Shore. Famed Virginia oysters from estate beds, served in its octagonal oyster house, supplement the hospitality of the mansion, a restored colonial residence with such amenities as a "natatorium" (indoor pool) and a fully-paneled tavern.

"BEAUREGARD" Brandy Station, Virginia

This historic farm was the site of the greatest cavalry engagement of the Civil War, the Battle of Brandy Station. A model farm of the Virginia Soil Conservation Program since 1946, in the heart of the Warrenton hunt country, this highly desirable 875-acre property with expertly restored 19th-century manor house is one of the largest and most productive farms within commuting distance of Washington, D.C.

MENLOUGH Warrenton, Virginia

The town of Warrenton is renowned as the capital of Virginia's Piedmont, the fabled hunt country of this historic state. Long known as one of Warrenton's great estates, Menlough is a superb property for the sportsman or the investor. Less than 50 miles from Washington, D.C., the offering encompasses one of the largest tracts of land within Warrenton, its 55 acres offering excellent development potential.

"WILD GOOSE HOUSE" Chestnut Hill, Pennsylvania

This charming country estate, situated on 7 secluded acres of splendidly landscaped property, includes a lovely meadow and stream with waterfall and a fine stand of trees that serve as a backdrop for the 21-room residence. Designed by Marmaduke Tilden in 1921 and located just beyond the Philadelphia city line, the limestone and cedar residence is a fine example of American craftsmanship, durability and traditional elegance.

Southeast

The Southeast—the heart of what has come to be called the "New South"—is a region of contrasts. The old agrarian South, with its vast estates and grand plantation homes, still survives in places like "Oaklawn," near Franklin, Louisiana, the site of Civil War battles and later a movie location where the grounds and a gracious 1837 manor house were recently sold for well over $1,000,000 by Sotheby Parke Bernet Realty. Fashionable winter resorts in Florida continue to attract the wealthy from all over the world to extraordinary properties such as a Boca Raton waterside estate which recently sold for over $660,000, an elegant Georgian-style residence in a fine location on prestigious John's Island, or one of a number of exquisite Palm Beach residences. But today's South, in the midst of a period of unparalleled economic expansion, offers townhouses in Miami or New Orleans as sought-after year-round residences as well as vacation homes or investment opportunities; improved transportation has changed large rural estates into more than simply leisure-time retreats. As a result, the market for luxury real estate in the Southeast is on firmer ground than ever before.

Sotheby Parke Bernet has taken a particularly active role in spurring the south's great tradition of the sporting estate. The 916-acre Weil Farm in Kentucky's famed Bluegrass country represents a once-in-a-lifetime opportunity to become a part of the finest horse breeding area in the world, while White Hall and Cherokee Plantations in South Carolina's hospitable "Lowcountry" are beautiful settings for waterfowl and upland game shooting. The Howe House in Pinehurst, North Carolina, is as close to paradise as a golfer can go.

Latin Americans and Canadians, as well as buyers from Europe and the United States, are leading the charge on real estate in the great Florida winter colonies. Rodney J. Dillard, who heads Sotheby's southeast real estate office in Palm Beach, reports that the luxury real estate market is operating at its highest volume in years, with significant appreciation in values. An elegant Regency-style villa and a stunning contemporary residence, both on Lake Worth, or a lushly landscaped villa designed by Clarence Mack, minutes from Worth Avenue are only a few of the extraordinary Palm Beach offerings Sotheby's has sold.

The Virgin Islands, the Bahamas, and selected portions of the Caribbean have recently experienced a resurgence of investment interest after a four or five year lull. In the Bahamas, Sotheby Parke Bernet is offering an undeveloped 80-acre parcel lined with coconut palms on the northern end of Windermere Island near Eleuthera, and has sold a 415-acre estate with a mile of Atlantic beachfront and a Bahamanian colonial residence—the largest sale in the Bahamas in recent memory.

CHEROKEE PLANTATION Yemassee, South Carolina

This plantation of more than 3,700 acres is one of the most magnificent in South Carolina's "Lowcountry," renowned for its farms and fine shooting estates. The richly detailed and superbly proportioned 1931 Georgian residence incorporates an 18th Century house reminiscent of the James River mansions, yet is modern in every respect, epitomizing the hospitality for which this region is justly famous.

WHITE HALL PLANTATION Yemassee, South Carolina

This 340-acre farm and sporting estate is truly one of the most charming and welcoming of the "Lowcountry" plantations. In a land of live oaks, Spanish moss, rivers and wildlife between Charleston and Savannah, the traditional plantation residence and its full complement of outbuildings make a delightful home for any sportsman or lover of the South Carolina countryside.

THE HOWE HOUSE
Pinehurst, North Carolina (*opposite*)

Situated in Pinehurst, one of America's best known resorts and its "golfing capital," this fine residence offers a perfect retreat from today's fast-paced lifestyle. Constructed largely from rustic and maintenance-free cypress, this home is on a lushly landscaped four acres in the larger 175-acre Clarendon Gardens.

THE WEIL FARM Paris, Kentucky

Situated on the Paris Pike, the finest location in Lexington's famed Bluegrass country, this 916-acre farm presents a unique opportunity to the world's horse breeders. Seldom is such a large tract of land, exemplifying in soil and terrain the best of Kentucky's farms, made available on the market, especially in this coveted area near internationally celebrated Claiborne, Greentree and Calumet Farms.

CHRETIEN POINT St. Landry Parish, Louisiana

Listed on the National Register of Historic Places and part of a land grant to Louis St. Germaine by the Spanish governor de Galvez in 1776, this beautiful antebellum estate is one of bayou country's best loved plantation properties—rich in history, romance and the gracious elegance of a bygone era.

A PALLADIAN VILLA Palm Beach, Florida

One of the most exquisite and meticulously maintained Palm Beach estates, this Clarence Mack residence is a study in classical elegance. Known for its fine collection of antiques auctioned by Sotheby Parke Bernet in New York, the beautifully detailed villa is set amidst lush gardens and secluded by high ficus hedges.

BAYFRONT ESTATE Coral Gables, Florida

A magnificent 4-acre property offering all the best of Southern Florida: a unique location in Gables Estates on the shores of Biscayne Bay with sweeping views across the water, frontage on a waterway off the Bay providing sheltered dockage for two boats, a tennis court and beautiful pool area, and a splendid sun-drenched residence reflecting the care and attention given to the entire property by its present owners.

PALM BEACH CLASSIC
Palm Beach, Florida (*opposite*)

One of the finest contemporary homes in Palm Beach makes extensive use of glass to bring its exquisitely landscaped Lake Worth setting into a spacious interior, highlighting the owner's extensive art collection. The result is a beautiful articulation of Palm Beach's modern lifestyle.

SADDLE CAY **Exuma Cays, Bahamas**

Midway in the chain of islands extending south from Nassau to Grand Exuma lies Saddle Cay. Few of the smaller Bahamian islands equal its presence and natural beauty as it rises out of the sea to an elevation of eighty feet, with fine sand beaches and coconut, ironwood and buttonwood trees. From the main house overlooking a 600-foot crescent of sandy beach, the vista includes most of the island's 90 acres, the surrounding islands and the Atlantic. Along one of the numerous beaches that ring the island is a deep-water channel making access possible by boat and there is also an airstrip on Norman's Cay, immediately to the south.

95

ELEGANT JOHN'S ISLAND RESIDENCE
John's Island, Florida

Designed by architect James E. Gibson, with interior design by Albert Hadley, this outstanding Georgian-style residence is situated in one of this exclusive resort community's choicest locations. Known for its miles of beautiful beaches and its unparalleled club facilities, John's Island and this superb residence with adjoining octagonal guest house and pool create the ultimate vacation paradise.

MEDITERRANEAN VILLA Palm Beach, Florida

White-washed brick, vine-covered wrought iron gates and a cloistered courtyard brimming with sunlight and lush vegetation set the Mediterranean mood of this charming residence, located just minutes from the shops of Worth Avenue and the ocean.

WATERSIDE RESIDENCE
Boca Raton, Florida (*top*)

This spacious property provides the ultimate in Southern Florida living. Situated on the grounds of the Royal Palm Yacht and Country Club with waterfrontage on Buccaneer Palm Waterway, this attractive residence is an in-town estate enjoying all the advantages of its country club location; a present-day testament to the plans of Addison Mizner in patterning his world-famed Boca Raton after Venice.

REGENCY VILLA
Palm Beach, Florida

In its private Parc Monceau setting terraced above Lake Worth, this exquisite Regency-style home achieves on an intimate scale the formal elegance of a grand Palm Beach estate.

UNICORN CAY Eleuthera, The Bahamas

One of the most important properties recently sold in the Bahamas, this 415-acre estate boasts almost a mile of Atlantic beachfront. Situated on one of the highest points of Eleuthera, the impressive Bahamian colonial residence, originally built for British author Rosita Forbes, commands breathtaking views of a tropical haven of beauty and privacy.

CARIBBEAN RETREAT
Windermere Island, The Bahamas *(right)*

Clear Bahamian waters and unspoiled white sand beaches lined with coconut palms border 80 undeveloped acres on the northern end of Windermere Island. One of the finest and most private properties in an area noted for its lifestyle of understated elegance, the property could be developed as a grand estate or divided into several attractive villa sites, providing a rare opportunity for investment in an exclusive tropical location.

OAKLAWN MANOR Franklin, Louisiana

Built on the site of Civil War battles, this historic 1837 planta-tion boasts one of the most dramatic classical mansions in the South. Oaklawn, with its manicured grounds on picturesque Bayou Teche, has been selected on several occasions as a filming location for a major motion picture.

IBIS ISLAND APARTMENT Palm Beach, Florida

Featured in *Architectural Digest* in 1975, this penthouse apartment affords spectacular views both toward the Atlantic and over Lake Worth and the Intracoastal Waterway. A haven of tranquility in the middle of Lake Worth, Ibis Island is a serene setting for an exclusive residence minutes from the heart of Palm Beach.

ST. CHARLES AVENUE RESIDENCE
New Orleans, Louisiana

On one of New Orleans' most prestigious residential streets, in the exclusive university section, this impeccably-maintained Louis XV-style mansion is unique not only for its location, but for its quality construction and lavish interior detail as well. Beautifully crafted woods, marble mantels, onyx baths and oak parquet floors lend an air of extraordinary elegance to the residence—a fitting address for a top executive and an ideal setting for elegant entertaining.

DUMAINE STREET TOWNHOUSE
New Orleans, Louisiana

Embodying the history and special flavor of old New Orleans, this historic townhouse is located in the heart of the renowned French Quarter, convenient to Royal Street shopping, the jazz of Bourbon Street and the gracious ambience of the Vieux Carré. Built in 1830, the 2½-story French Creole townhouse was meticulously renovated a few years ago to accommodate all modern amenities as well as several income-producing apartments, making the residence a splendid pied-à-terre for a corporation or a frequent visitor to New Orleans.

The West

The western half of the "Sun Belt" has experienced enormous growth in recent years, its warm climate, favorable tax structure and lower energy costs attracting individuals and corporations from across the nation and abroad. Not surprisingly, luxury residential real estate in all areas of the west has enjoyed "boom times" as well. Many new residents are settling in to the easy-going western lifestyle and finding it accords beautifully with the expansive properties offered for sale by Sotheby Parke Bernet Realty; other newcomers to the fast-paced cities of Houston, Dallas and Los Angeles are searching for the sanctuary and comfort of elegant in-town properties.

Values in luxury western properties seem to survive most fluctuations in the economy. The term "luxury," however, varies by area. Dallas, where real estate is enjoying excellent growth both in town and in the suburbs, remains a largely untapped market. According to Susan Marcus of Erle Rawlins Realtors this luxury category starts in the $250,000 range. In Los Angeles, it often refers to properties valued at well over $1 million. Houston, the energy capital of America, has a strong executive home market. According to John Daugherty, the city's foremost residential realtor, Houston's established areas such as River Oaks and the contemporary Memorial district

have strong markets with escalating prices responding to diminishing supply and growing demand. Texans are looking for an exchange or addition of properties, foreigners are interested in American investment or residency, and new residents are moving in to take advantage of Houston's burgeoning economy and contagious dynamism.

In Los Angeles and throughout all of Southern California, the luxury real estate market is currently undergoing a similar though perhaps more widely publicized boom, destined to move out of a brief lull with an influx of Europeans looking for farms and ranches, Middle and Far Easterners in search of the finely manicured estates of Bel Air and Beverly Hills, and the continued interest of show business people and wealthy professionals. One of Sotheby Parke Bernet's most noteworthy sales in this area was that of a widely acclaimed contemporary residence overlooking the Pacific Coast in Montecito, recently purchased by a popular new comedian. In Palm Springs, famed for its dry desert climate and meticulously maintained golf courses, Sotheby's is offering a striking desert contemporary overlooking the green fairways of the Thunderbird Country Club.

Sotheby Parke Bernet Realty also specializes in the sale of luxury western ranch estates such as Five Angels, a romantic 7,000-acre hideaway in the heart of an Arizona desert nature preserve and "Cielo," an 84-acre guest ranch twenty minutes from Dallas, ideal for a filming location, corporate retreat or country club and already equipped with a golf course, tennis court, theatre building and heliport.

CENTRAL TEXAS ESTATE Bryan, Texas

This elegant Greek Revival-style residence, unquestionably the finest in all of Brazos County, is surrounded by grounds landscaped by Peter Michele of Dallas. Located at the edge of a dense forest in a rapidly growing region near Texas A & M University, the property offers all the advantages of small town living, yet is less than one hour from both Houston and Dallas by air.

RIVER OAKS RESIDENCE Houston, Texas

This simple, yet elegantly styled contemporary residence enjoys easy access to the active life of one of America's fastest-growing, most exciting and economically viable cities, while at the same time providing a luxurious wooded retreat in Houston's premier residential community, minutes from downtown.

MADEWOOD Houston, Texas

This mansion is designed in the gracious style of an antebellum plantation home. Modeled after Madewood, a Louisiana manor, the elegant residence combines the charm of a Southern estate with the convenience of an attractive in-town location.

JACK RABBIT HILL Kerrville, Texas

In the famed Texas hill country, birthplace of the late President Lyndon B. Johnson, this charming residence with its special garden setting, designed by C. C. Fleming, noted international landscape architect, interior designer and planning consultant, enjoys commanding views over the imposing Guadalupe River Valley from its majestic hilltop setting.

#18 COURTLANDT PLACE Houston, Texas

Located on historic Courtlandt Place amidst the Victorian splendor of turn-of-the-century homes, this finely constructed residence is in Houston's oldest restricted residential neighborhood. Built in 1910 by William T. Carter Jr., this attractive Spanish-Prairie style home was lovingly restored by Mr. Carter's grandson in 1975.

"TREETOPS" Houston, Texas

This superb contemporary residence, soon to be featured in *Architectural Digest*, makes extensive use of glass in every room to provide spectacular views of a lush central atrium, numerous courtyards, and a secluded pool and garden. Set in a lovely wooded area, "Treetops" is one of the finest new estates in River Oaks, one of Houston's most exclusive residential districts.

MEMORIAL CONTEMPORARY Houston, Texas

This extraordinary contemporary home provides the ultimate in spaciousness and modern convenience and is ideally suited for large-scale sophisticated entertainment. With a 153-foot serpentine pool in the extravagant rear grounds, this monumentally-scaled residence is located among many distinguished homes in the woods of Farnham Park, one of the city's most desirable neighborhoods.

"CIELO" Dallas, Texas

A unique gentleman's ranch one-half hour from Dallas, this 84-acre property is ideally suited for a corporate retreat or country club with its superb setting on Lake Dallas and accommodations for entertaining up to 1,000 guests. A variety of recreational facilities including golf, tennis, and swimming are offered on the property, and with nearly 8,000 feet of lake frontage, all watersports are near at hand. Outstanding improvements on the ranch include a heliport and grass landing strip, as well as a theatre and movie set.

THE CURTIS MANSION
Belton, Texas (*opposite*)

In a lovely recreational area ringed with heavily wooded hills and with two freshwater lakes nearby, this stately Edwardian residence is a beautifully preserved Texas landmark, located just sixty miles north of Austin.

FIVE ANGELS RANCH Sonoita, Arizona

This romantic Arizona ranch hideaway is presently owned by Harding Lawrence, chairman of Braniff Airways, and his wife Mary Wells, chairman of the advertising firm of Wells, Rich, Greene, Inc. Reminiscent of a Tuscan hill town, the multi-level contemporary ranch house hugs the side of a hill commanding 150 deeded acres on a mile-high plateau in the foothills of the Huachuca Mountains. The property is surrounded by a 7,000-acre perpetually wild desert nature preserve.

DESERT RESORT ESTATE Palm Springs, California

This exceptional stone, glass and marble contemporary, with its exquisite terraced grounds and towering palms, contrasts vividly against a backdrop of desert and the pine-covered San Jacinto Mountains. Situated on the grounds of the Thunderbird Country Club, this extraordinary estate, featured in *Architectural Digest,* is in fact its own self-contained resort, with professional tennis court, black marble pool and outdoor marble dance floor.

MONTECITO CONTEMPORARY Santa Barbara, California

Since its completion in 1974, this powerful house has acquired a reputation as one of the most important residences recently built in California. Designed by architect Roland Coate Jr., the contemporary masterpiece, recently purchased by a well known comedian, is set into the crest of a hillside in fabled Montecito, with sweeping views of mountains and the sea.

Index

NEW ENGLAND

The Richmond House
Woodstock, Vermont   *Sold*
18 mi. W of Hanover, N.H., 125 mi. to Boston, 2 in-town acres w/ 100 ft. on Ottauquechee River. 10-bdr. brick residence c. 1826, in excel. condition. Servant's/rental apt. Furn. negotiable. *Local Agent: Georgina Williamson*, 23 The Green, Woodstock 05091, tel. 802/457-2760.

The Yellow House
Wilton Center, New Hampshire   *$225,000*
1 hr. N. of Boston, 15 wooded acres, 1800's Federal-style wood frame residence (6 bdrs./6 bths.) modernized in '64 w/ 6-room apt. wing. 5-story barn/carriage house. *Local Agent: The Petersons, Inc.*, Realtors, 42 Grove St., Peterborough, N.H. 03458, tel. 603/924-3321.

Dionis Beach Estate
Nantucket, Massachusetts   *Sold*
3 mi. from Nantucket, 1 hr. by air to N.Y.C., 11 acres w/ 670-ft. beach on Sound. 6-bdr. wood frame residence; 4-bdr. staff cottage; stable; beach house w/ fireplace, 2 bths. *Local Agent: Land/Vest, Inc.*, 14 Kilby St., Boston 02109, tel. 617/723-1800.

Elm Hill Farm
Clarendon, Vermont   *$425,000*
5 mi. from Rutland w/ daily flts. to Boston, 575 acres run as small dairying operation. 9-bdr. 1780's colonial residence; 7 major outbuildings. 20 min. to ski areas. *Local Agent: Roland Beers & Associates*, Manchester, Vt. 05254, tel. 802/362-1838.

Oceanfront Summer Residence
Watch Hill, Rhode Island   *$325,000*.
2½ hrs. to N.Y.C., 20 mi. to New London, Ct. 2½ oceanfront acres w/ 360-ft. beach. 1920's 11-bdr./ 9-bth. wood frame residence w/ apt; bath house. Furn. negotiable. *Local Agent: Gustave J. S. White, Inc.*, 37 Bellevue Ave., Newport 02840, tel. 401/847-4200.

Oceanfront Development
Cape Rosier, Maine   *$1,150,000*
4 mi. N.E. of Dark Harbor, 50 min. by air to Boston. 412 unimproved acres w/ 2½-mi. shoreline on ocean. Rare depth of water (198 ft. w/in 300 ft. of shore) allows wide range of development possibilities. Year-round road access. *Local agent: C. R. deRochemont*, Realtor, 106 Pleasant St., Rockland, Me. 04841, tel. 207/594-8124.

The Proctor House
Boston, Massachusetts   *Sold*
On Beacon St., 5-story Greek Revival-style townhouse c. 1825, in excel. condition. 6 bdrs./6 bths; walled garden courtyard; deeded parking space. *Local Agent: Hunneman & Co., Inc.*, 16 Arlington St., Boston 02116, tel. 617/266-4430.

"Chailey"
Newburyport, Massachusetts   *Sold*
35 min. to Boston, 20-acre estate w/ 1700 ft. on Merrimack River; heated pool; stable: gazebo; garages. 15-room (7 bdrs., staff rooms) Georgian-style residence c. 1892; prize-winning gardens. *Local Agent: Hunneman & Co., Inc.*, 21 Green St., Newburyport 01950, tel. 617/462-4430.

Hammersmith Farm
Newport, Rhode Island   *Sold*
2 hrs. from Boston, 55-acre waterfront estate (can support cattle) on Narragansett Bay w/ 575-ft. frontage. 10-bdr./12-bth. 1887 summer cottage; 5-bdr./ 4-car carriage house; farm buildings. 10 staff bdrs. *Local Agent: Gustave J. S. White, Inc.*, 37 Bellevue Ave., Newport 02840, tel. 401/847-4200.

The Anchorage
Seal Harbor, Maine   *Sold*
3-acre promontory on S.W. shore, 40-min. flt. to Boston. Overlooking sea, 8-bdr. (each w/ fireplace) frame & stone residence. Terraces, decks, balconies. Ample staff & guest bdrs. Heated saltwater pool. *Local Agent: Dwight B. Carter*, Northeast Harbor, Me. 04662, tel. 207/276-5458 (or) *The Knowles Company*, Northeast Harbor, Me. 04662, tel. 207/276-3322.

"Shangri-La"
Yarmouth, Nova Scotia, Canada *$1,950,000*
On 2 islands, 40 min. by air to Boston, 582-acre hunting preserve w/ 7-mi. oceanfrontage. 11,000 sq. ft. main lodge w/ indoor pool, gym, staff apt., 2 guest houses; barns. Unrestricted building rights/ Canadian gov't. development incentives. *Local Agent: L. G. Trask Agency Ltd.*, 396 Main St., Yarmouth B5A 1E9, tel. 902/742-3535, telex: 019-38522.

"Saheda"
                                    $600,000
Seal Harbor, Maine   *(furnished)*
½-mi. from Seal Harbor Yacht Club, 4½ acres w/ 875-ft. oceanfrontage. 9-room steel/granite/cypress contemp. on granite cliffs 60 ft. above sea. 5 bdrs./ 4½ bths. Fine Amer. & Eur. furnishings. *Local Agent: Robert E. Garrity*, Northeast Harbor, Me. 04662, tel. 207/276-5851.

Prospect Farm
Sherborn, Massachusetts   *Sold*
18 mi. from Boston, 38 wooded acres; formal gardens, stream, pond. 9-room country house on foundation of 19th-Cent. barn, 3 bdrs./3 bths. Pool; cabana. Near excel. schools, clubs. *Local Agent: Homer Associates*, 5 Washington St:, Sherborn 01770, tel. 617/653-7599.

Wheelbarrow Hill
Great Barrington, Massachusetts *$1,100,000*
3 mi. S. of Great Barrington, 2½ hrs. to N.Y.C. or Boston, 300 acres (125 corn/hay). 16-room residence (4 bdrs./5½ bths./serv. qtrs.); 2-bdr. guest house; contemp. poolhouse w/ liv. accomd; pool, pond, stables. *Local Agent: Albert Borden, Inc.*, Main St., Lakeville, Ct. 06039, tel. 203/435-2400.

Vaucluse Farm
Portsmouth, Rhode Island   *Sold*
10 min. from Newport, 70 min. from Boston, 230 acres (175 tillable) ½-acre S.F.H. zoned w/ good road frontage, 2100 ft. on Sakonnet River. Georgian-style mansion (11 bdrs./3 staff rooms); 6-barn farm complex; mgr.'s, staff houses; greenhouses. *Local Agent: Gustave J. S. White*, 37 Bellevue Ave., Newport 02840, tel. 401/847-4200.

Rockland Farm
South Dartmouth, Massachusetts   *$750,000*
                                  on 6 acres.
5 mi. S. of New Bedford, 1 hr. to Boston, 10 acres w/ 175 ft. on Buzzard's Bay. 4-bdr. wood frame, stone & glass contemp. w/ indoor pool. Guest house; tennis court; bowling alley. 2 adjoining 2-acre lots avail. *Local Agent: Vera J. Almgren*, 40 School St., South Dartmouth 02748, tel. 617/994-5622.

Martha's Vineyard Contemporary
Chilmark, Massachusetts   *$225,000*.
On Vineyard, 3 acres on Prospect Hill, 5-bdr. white cedar shingle contemp. Spectacular views, beaut. maintained. Skylights, decks, 16-ft. ceilings. *Local Agent: Barbara Nevin Real Estate*, Upper Main St., Edgartown, Mass. 02439, tel. 617/627-4041.

NORTHEAST

featured on cover:

"Landfall"
Princeton, New Jersey $1,350,000
3 mi. from Univ., 50 mi. from N.Y.C., on 23 buildable acres (2-acre S.F.H. zoned) 8-bdr./7-bth. Norman/Tudor residence w/ 7 fireplaces, in excel. condition. Garage w/ 3-bdr. mgr.s apt., artist's studio, wine cellar. Pool. *Local Agent: Calloway Realty*, 4 Nassau St., Princeton 08540, tel. 809/921-1050.

Crow's Nest
Fishers Island, New York $350,000
Estate section of island, 2 hrs. from N.Y.C., on 10 acres w/ 8-bdr./8-bth. wood frame cedar & oak house built in '27. Fully winterized, 6 fireplaces; magnif. views over water. *Sotheby Parke Bernet International Realty*, 980 Madison Ave., N.Y.C. 10021, tel. 212/472-3465.

Medieval Seaside Castle
Fishers Island, New York *Sold*
E. Point peninsula of island, 2 hrs. from N.Y.C., 6½ acres w/ views of Ct., R.I., L.I; 2,000-ft. water-frontage. 20-room Brittany-style castle, modernized in '70s w/ 6 bdrs., 2 guest suites; stone garage building. Furnished. *Sotheby Parke Bernet International Realty*, 980 Madison Ave., N.Y.C. 10021, tel. 212/472-3465.

Quaker Hill Stock Farm
Pawling, New York *Sold*
65 mi. from N.Y.C., 282-acre working farm (2 parcels, w/ 247 acres pasture/cropland) operated for dairy cow, horse breeding. Fine colonial residence (5 bdrs./5 bths.); pool house. Mgr.'s house, barns, farm buildings. *Sotheby Parke Bernet International Realty*, 980 Madison Ave., N.Y.C. 10021, tel. 212/472-3465

Aknusti Estate
$875,000
Delaware County, New York *(partially furn.)*
3½ hrs. from N.Y.C., 1839-acre horse & game farm w/ 350 acres crop & pasture, high timber value in 1400 acres; streams, ponds. Estate house w/ 9 bdrs., each w/ bath; servant's wing. Stable complex; game farm. *Sotheby Parke Bernet International Realty*, 980 Madison Ave., N.Y.C. 10021, tel. 212/472-3465.

Bonnie Brae Farm
Millbrook, New York $600,000
80 mi. from N.Y.C., on 171 acres (25 acres cropland, 10 acres paddocks) w/ show ring & 3-acre pond. 2-story frame colonial house w/ 5 bdrs; farm manager's house; bank barn. Zoned 10-acre residential. *Local Agent: George T. Whalen, Inc.*, Franklin Ave., Millbrook 12545, tel. 914/667-3434.

Clove Creek Farm
Poughquag, New York $2,500,000
90 min. from N.Y.C., 560-acre beef cattle farm (hay & corn silage for cattle, horses & sheep grown on property) w/ 6-bdr./6-bth. colonial c. 1812, renov. in '30s; staff qtrs. Farm buildings; stable complex; mgr.'s & guest houses. Acreage 80% tillable

w/ ample water; 2-acre S.F.H.-zoned. *Sotheby Parke Bernet International Realty*, 980 Madison Ave., N.Y.C. 10021, tel. 212/472-3465.

Quarry Lake
Northcastle, New York $750,000
Central Westchester, 45 min. from N.Y.C., 45 fenced acres w/ 2-acre, 85-ft.-deep spring-fed quarry lake; tennis court; bathhouse on beach; 3-bdr. mgr.'s cottage; garage w/ staff apt.; stable; generator building. 5-bdr./7½-bth. French Provincial-style residence in excel. cond. *Sotheby Parke Bernet International Realty*, 980 Madison Ave., N.Y.C. 10021, tel. 212/472-3465.

Valley Castle
Cornwall, Connecticut $850,000
In Litchfield Hills, less than 100 mi. to Hartford or N.Y., 258 acres, 80% wooded w/ streams, ponds. Castle-like residence built in '20s (7 bdrs./10 bths.), renov. in '65. 5 stone dwellings; 9 other outbuildings; stables. *Sotheby Parke Bernet International Realty*, 980 Madison Ave., N.Y.C. 10021, tel. 212/472-3465

"Hobby Barn"
Pound Ridge, New York *Sold*
1-hr. drive to N.Y.C., 7 wooded acres w/ pond, beaut. gardens. 150-year-old barn reconstructed in '60s w/ 3 bdrs., 5 bths, staff apt; pool. *In House & Garden. Local Agent: A. T. Houlihan*, 83 S. Greely Avenue, Chappaqua, N.Y. 10514, tel. 914/238-4766.

"New Pond"
Carmel, New York $550,000
89.2 richly wooded acres, 90 min. from N.Y.C., w/ 5-bdr. frame & stone contemp. residence, in excel. condition, overlooks private 9-acre pond. Pool; cabana; 3-bdr. guest house; garage; boat house. *Sotheby Parke Bernet International Realty*, 980 Madison Ave., N.Y.C. 10021, tel. 212/472-3465.

"Seascape"
Locust, New Jersey $900,000
Near Rumson, 1¼ hrs. from N.Y.C., on 39 acres overlooking Navesink River w/ocean beyond, 19-room brick Georgian built in '29 w/ 7 master bdrs. Pool, paddocks, stable, greenhouse. *Sotheby Parke Bernet International Realty*, 980 Madison Ave., N.Y.C. 10021, tel. 212/472-3465.

The Harkness Estate
Snedens Landing, New York *Sold*
On Palisades, 40 min. from mid-town, 7.45 heavily wooded acres w/ 650-ft. frontage on Hudson. 30-room main house w/ 6 master suites, 7 servant's rooms, 14 bths; ballroom/dance studio wing; pool. *Sotheby Parke Bernet International Realty*, 980 Madison Ave., N.Y.C. 10021, tel. 212/472-3465.

Cooper's Bluff Contemporary
Cove Neck, Long Island, New York *Sold*
6.5 acres on peninsula of Cooper's Bluff, 30 min. to N.Y. airports, w/yachting, tennis, golf nearby. Multi-sectional contemp. 160 ft. above water (5 bdrs./5½ bths./ staff rooms); pool house w/living accomd. 1200 ft. on Oyster Bay Harbor. *Local Agent: Foxpoint, Ltd.*, 82 Birch Hill Rd., Locust Valley, N.Y. 11560, tel. 516/671-6110.

"Tirranna"
New Canaan, Connecticut $1,500,000
1 hr. from N.Y.C., 13 beaut. landscaped acres w/ 1956–58 Frank Lloyd Wright mahogany & glass residence overlooking pool, pond, spillway & jet fountain; pool house; staff wing. Some Wright built-ins & furnishings incl. *Local Agent: William Pitt, Inc.*, 50 Post Road W., Westport, Ct. 06880, tel. 203/227-1246.

Reynwood
Greenwich, Connecticut *Sold*
46.4 wooded acres, 4-acre S.F.H. zoned, 45 min. to N.Y.C. Stone manor house w/ 8 bdrs., 7 bths., 3 half bths., serv. rooms. Stable, caretaker's cottage; pool, pond, paddocks. *Local Agent: New England Land Co., Ltd.*, 783 North St., Greenwich 06830, tel. 203/869-8001.

Lord's Cove Retreat
Old Lyme, Connecticut *Sold*
25.8 acres w/ ¼-mi. frontage on Conn. River estuary, 2 hrs. from N.Y. or Boston. 14-room Colonial-style house; 2-bdr. guest house, greenhouse, boat house; pool. *Local Agent: The Dunham Company*, Realtors, 1 Davis Rd. W., Old Lyme 06371, tel. 203/434-9100.

"Lochmere"
Little Silver, New Jersey $590,000
13 acres in Rumson area, luxury seaside community 50 mi. from N.Y.C., w/ 1400 ft. on S. Shrewsbury River, 7-bdr./6½-bth. 3-story residence w/ newly-built poolhouse wing; tennis court; 60-ft. pool. All in excel. cond. *Local Agent: Applebrook Agency*, 950 Highway #35, Middletown, N.J. 07748, tel. 201/671-2300.

Spectacular Contemporary Residence
Alpine, New Jersey $2,500,000
On 6 acres 20 min. to N.Y.C., 15,000-sq. ft. Norman Jaffe contemporary built in '76 in 3 wings (entertainment/family/recreation) w/ magnif. indoor pool; master suite w/ private atrium, 2 dress. rooms, 2 bths; 4 add'l family bdrs; staff apt., Custom built-ins throughout. *Sotheby Parke Bernet International Realty*, 980 Madison Ave., N.Y.C. 10021, tel. 212/472-3465.

"Rio Vista"
Alpine & Cresskill, New Jersey *Sold*
5 mi. N. of G.W. Bridge, in Palisades area, 292.4 acres, 100% buildable; 1, 1½, 2-acre S.F.H. zoned. Favorable tax climate, excellent schools nearby. *Sotheby Parke Bernet International Realty*, 980 Madison Ave., N.Y.C. 10021, tel. 212/472-3465.

MANHATTAN

820 Fifth Avenue *New York City* *Sold*
Full floor, nearly 10,000 sq. ft. w/ windows on 4 exp., teak parquet floors, eleg. wall coverings. 18 rooms: 4 bdrs. + study, each w/ bth., 3 staff rooms. Gourmet kit., wine closet. Intercom, parking, good security. *Sotheby Parke Bernet International Realty*, 980 Madison Avenue, N.Y.C. 10021, tel. 212/472-3465.

Contemporary Maisonette
New York City $695,000 (for both apts.).
Sutton Pl. at 58th St., mod. building, 2 adjacent apts., each w/ sidewalk & lobby entry. Apt A: 7 rooms w/ unique built-ins, concealed doors, mirrored walls, lux. details. Apt. B: Smaller, ideal for office/guest suite w/ liv. and din. rooms. *Sotheby Parke Bernet International Realty*, 980 Madison Ave., N.Y.C. 10021, tel. 212/472-3465.

Murray Hill Townhouse
New York City *Sold*
38th St., E. of Park Ave. Decorator-designed 5-story townhouse renov. in '76 w/ conservatory, rear garden. Built-in stereo, central a/c, burglar alarm. 4 bdrs., staff rooms. Income-producing potential. *Sotheby Parke Bernet International Realty*, 980 Madison Ave., N.Y.C. 10021, tel. 212/472-3465.

Contemporary Collector's Residence
New York City *Sold*
E. 79th St., off Park, full-floor apt. w/ windows on 4 exp. 14 rooms, 3 WBF's. Master suite w/ 2 bths., 3 add'l. bdrs. Staff qtrs., chauffeur rooms. Renov. in '75, in *House & Garden*. *Sotheby Parke Bernet International Realty*, 980 Madison Avenue, N.Y.C. 10021, tel. 212/472-3465.

Jacobean Duplex
New York City *Sold*
57th St., near Sutton Pl., 6-room duplex w/ extens. oak paneling, 19½-ft. ceils., gourmet kit., wine cellar. 2 large master bdrs., each w/ bth. Offered partially furn. *Sotheby Parke Bernet International Realty*, 980 Madison Ave., N.Y.C. 10021, tel. 212/472-3465.

Stately Apartment Residence
New York City *Sold*
4 E. 72nd St., 11-room co-op apt., fully renov. w/ windows on 4 exp. 4 bdrs., 2 maid's rooms, 3 WBF's. Built-in stereo; gourmet kit; a/c. *Sotheby Parke Bernet International Realty*, 980 Madison Ave., N.Y.C. 10021, tel. 212/472-3465.

Palazzo Triplex *New York City* *Sold*
E. 50's, on river, 9th, 10th, 11th-floor apt. 4 bdrs./5 bths., staff rooms. 2-story ballroom by Jansen, Inc., gourmet kit., dumbwaiter, elevator, built-in stereo, intercom, wine closet. *Sotheby Parke Bernet International Realty*, 980 Madison Avenue, N.Y.C. 10021, tel. 212/472-3465.

Sutton Place Residence
New York City *Sold*
#1 Sutton Pl. S., overlooks river & gardens. 13 rooms (3 bdrs./4 bths.) w/ servant's qtrs; In excel. cond. 3 fireplaces, 10½-ft. ceils., marble floors, 18th-C. murals, Clarence House wallcoverings. *Sotheby Parke Bernet International Realty*, 980 Madison Avenue, N.Y.C. 10021, tel. 212/472-3465.

Philip Johnson Townhouse
New York City *Sold*
E. 52nd St., 2 stories (plus cellar), orig. 1860's carriage house, reconstructed in '49 as guest house,

Liv. area & master suite separated by glass-walled terraced water garden. Guest room, library upstairs. *Sotheby Parke Bernet International Realty*, 980 Madison Avenue, N.Y.C. 10021, tel. 212/472-3465.

MID-ATLANTIC

Country Estate
Greenville, Delaware *Sold*
25 mi. from Philadelphia, 11½ acres w/ fenced paddocks, pasture, woodland; barn, stable, tack house. 5-bdr. colonial-style brick residence w/ rear patio/pool area; garage. *Local Agent: Patterson-Schwartz & Assoc., Inc.*, 913 Delaware Ave., Wilmington 19899, tel. 302/656-3141

Georgian Estate
Centerville, Delaware *Sold*
7 mi. from Wilmington, 25 mi. to Philadelphia, 40.7 acres (20 acres pasture) zoned 2-acre resid. 8-bdr. brick Georgian-style house; 18th C.-style paneling, 5 fireplaces throughout. Good schools, clubs nearby. *Local Agent: Patterson Schwartz & Assoc., Inc.*, 913 Delaware Ave., Wilmington 19899, tel. 302/656-3141.

"Tacaro"
Tracy's Landing, Maryland *Sold*
W. shore of Chesapeake Bay, 26 mi. from Washington, D.C., 388-acre (100 tillable) horse farm w/ Georgian-style manor house (7 bdrs., 12 bths.) w/ views to Bay; dairy, show, tobacco & horse barns (all brick); 7 tenant houses; smoke house. *Sotheby Parke Bernet International Realty*, 41 Culpeper St., Warrenton, Va. 22186, tel. 703/347-7577.

"Melfield"
Eastern Shore, Maryland *Sold*
1½ hrs. from Baltimore, Washington & Wilmington, 215 acres (wood fenced pasture & cropland) near junction of Chester & Corsica Rivers. Pre-Revolutionary colonial; guest house, servant's house, smokehouse; pool. *Local Agent: John H. Porter, Inc.*, 130 Washington St., Easton, Md. 21601, tel. 301/822-3117.

Edgehill Farm
Glyndon, Maryland $685,000
30 min. to Baltimore, 20 mi. to Baltimore/Washington airport, 87½-acre hunt country farm w/ fenced paddocks, 3 barns (44 stalls), two 3-bdr. tenant houses. 1920's 5-bdr. limestone residence w/ 5 fireplaces, greenhouse room, staff room w/ bth. *Sotheby Parke Bernet International Realty*, 41 Culpeper St., Warrenton, Va. 22186, tel. 703/347-7577.

"Belfield"
Lexington, Virginia *Sold*
Adjacent to Washington & Lee Univ., 2½ beaut. maint. acres w/ 1929 Norman/Tudor/Elizabethan-style house: 5 bdrs., 5½ bths., serv. qtrs. Renowned gardens. 3 hrs. to Washington. *Local Agent: Mead Associates*, 21 North Main St., Lexington 24450, tel. 703/463-7168.

"Little England"
Gloucester County, Virginia *Sold*
Near Williamsburg, 2½ hrs. from Washington, D.C., 62 acres on York River (1-mile shoreline) w/ 2 deep-water docks, pond, orchards, boxwood gardens. 7-bdr./7-bth. pre-Revolutionary plantation house, in superb cond.; brick pool house; 4-bdr. guest house; gardener's & mgr.'s houses; 14 add'l. farm buildings. *Local Agent: Jim & Pat Carter Real Estate*, P.O. Box 7, White Stone, Va. tel. 804/435-3131.

"Blenheim"
Charlottesville, Virginia *Sold*
115 mi. from Washington, 257-acre (100 open land) historic farm w/ 4-bdr. main residence dating to 1745. 3-bdr. guest house; schoolhouse/studio; atheneum; 2-bdr. mgr.'s house; chapel. *Local Agent: Stevens & Company*, One Boar's Head Pl., Charlottesville 22901, tel. 804/296-6104.

"Ednam"
Albemarle County, Virginia $1,500,000.
Charlottesville, near Univ. of Va., 35½ acres ideal for low-density devel. of high quality single-family homes. Rolling pasture & woodland, 580–673-ft. elevation. Victorian manor house, guest house, smoke house, stable. *Local Agent: Stevens & Company*, One Boar's Head Pl., Charlottesville 22901, tel. 804/296-6104.

Corbin Hall
Accomack County, Virginia *Sold*
Eastern Shore, 3½ hrs. to Washington, D.C., 470 acres (125 in cultivation) w/ ½-mile frontage on Chincoteague Bay. Georgian residence c. 1787, renov. in '70s: 4-bdrs., 6 fireplaces, beaut. paneling, hardwood floors. 3-bdr. guest house; stables; farm buildings. All in superb cond. *Sotheby Parke Bernet International Realty*, 41 Culpeper St., Warrenton, Va. 22186, tel. 703/347-7577.

The Meadow
Doswell, Caroline County, Virginia *Sold*
1½ hrs. from Washington, D.C., 2,652-acre horse breeding/training estate w/ 12 barns, mgr.'s residence, 7 staff houses; indoor/outdoor training tracks; 53 paddocks; ponds. 6-bdr. main residence w/ elev., wine cellar, staff qtrs; pool, tennis court. *Sotheby Parke Bernet International Realty*, 41 Culpeper St., Warrenton, Va. 22186, tel. 703/347-7577.

"Nanzatico"
King George County, Virginia *Sold*
75 mi. S. of Washington, D.C., 70½ acres (50 tillable) w/ 2,000 ft. on Rappahannock River. 3-bdr. National & Virginia Register colonial mansion; 2-bdr. guest house; several farm buildings. All in excel. cond. *Local Agent: Jim & Pat Carter Real Estate, Inc.*, P.O. Box 7, White Stone, Va. 22578, tel. 804/435-3131.

Eyreville
Cheriton, Virginia *Sold*
Eastern Shore, 5 hrs. from Washington, D.C., 1,022 acres (480 tilled, 20 oyster beds) fronting 6½ mi. of Chesapeake Bay. 6-bdr./7½-bth. 18th-C. Georgian; oyster house on water; kennel; garages; 5 tenant houses. Pond w/ underground irrigation,

beach, dock on Bay. *Sotheby Parke Bernet International Realty*, 41 Culpeper St., Warrenton, Va. 22186, tel. 703/347-7577.

"Beauregard"
Brandy Station, Virginia $1,950,000
1¼ hrs. from Washington, D.C., 875-acre beef cattle farm (490 cropland) in hunt country w/ 3 ponds, tennis court, several barn & tenant buildings. 7-bdr./6-bth. Southern Colonial, beaut. restored, 8 fireplaces. 3-mile frontage on state highways. *Sotheby Parke Bernet International Realty*, 41 Culpeper St., Warrenton, Va. 22186, tel. 703/347-7577.

"Menlough"
Warrenton, Virginia $925,000
1¼ hrs. from Washington, 55-acre in-town estate w/ excel. devel. potential (R-15 zoning). 5-bdr. Southern Colonial c. 1853 w/ indoor pool; kennel, stable, greenhouse; 1-bdr. cottage. Private airport nearby. *Sotheby Parke Bernet International Realty*, 41 Culpeper St., Warrenton, Va. 22186, tel. 703/347-7577.

"Wild Goose House"
Chestnut Hill, Pennsylvania $375,000
10 min. from Philadelphia city line, on 7 acres w/ meadow, stream, gardens & woods, 21-room limestone & cedar residence, in excel. cond.; guest/caretaker's house; pool, poolhouse. *Local Agent: Eichler & Moffly, Inc.*, Realtors, 97 Bethlehem Pike, Philadelphia, Pa. 19118. tel. 215/CH8-4050.

SOUTHEAST

Cherokee Plantation
Yemassee, South Carolina $3,500,000
Fronting 7 mi. on Combahee River, 3,727 contiguous acres (woodland, dyked rice fields, cropland, cypress swamp); 37 acres of ponds, canals; 13-acre lake. 11-bdr. Georgian-style mansion, serv. qtrs.; 3-bdr. mgr.'s house; 4-bdr. antebellum house; kennels, stable, garages. Livestock & farm equipment included. *Local Agent: William P. Baldwin*, P.O. Box 818, Summerville, S.C. 29483, tel. 803/873-2296.

White Hall Plantation
Yemassee, South Carolina $450,000
On Combahee River, near Charleston & Savannah, 340-acre (31, ricefield marsh; 79, wooded ricefields; 72, paddocks & pasture) horse/cattle farm. 19th-C. 5-bdr. plantation house; 14 outbuildings incl. 4-bdr. mgr.'s house, staff cottages, stables, barns, greenhouse. *Local Agent: William P. Baldwin*, P.O. Box 818, Summerville, S.C. 29483, tel. 803/873-2296.

The Howe House
Pinehurst, North Carolina $250,000
Sandshills area of Pinehurst, near golf & country clubs, 4 pine-wooded acres, magnif. landscaping in Clarendon Gardens, 10-bdr. cypress frame house, built in '29, 11 fireplaces, 2 staff rooms; garage. *Local Agent: Dale A. Hamlin*, P.O. Box 1627, Pinehurst, N.C. 28374, tel. 800/334-9530 or 919/295-6144.

The Weil Farm
Paris, Kentucky $5,954,845 ($6,500 per acre)
70 mi. from Louisville & Cincinnatti, 12 mi. E. of Lexington, on Paris-Lexington Pike, 916 calcium-rich acres (20 in tobacco) in Bluegrass region; 5 wells, irrigation lake, 5 ponds, stream. 2 residences; 7 barns adaptable to horses. Near major horse farms. *Local Agent: Doug Gibson Realtors*, 2025 Regency Road, Lexington 40503, tel. 606/278-9424.

Chretien Point
St. Landry Parish, Louisiana $1,100,000
15 min. from Lafayette, 4 hrs. to Houston, on 20 acres bordering Bayou Bourbeau, 10-room 1830's mansion w/ 6 WBF's, central a/c, 5 bdrs. In excel. cond. Pool, pond. *Local Agent: Farnsworth-Samuel, Ltd.* 1521 Washington Ave., New Orleans, La. 70115, tel. 504/891-6400.

A Palladian Villa
Palm Beach, Florida Sold
1.5 acres of lawn, fruit trees, tropical growth w/15-room single-level Clarence Mack-designed house w/3 bdrs. 3½ bths., staff qtrs., lavish pool pavilion/guest house. Central heat, a/c, alarm system. *Sotheby Parke Bernet International Realty Corp.*, Brokers, 155 Worth Ave., Palm Beach 33480, tel. 305/659-3555.

Bayfront Estate
Coral Gables, Florida $2,000,000
4 acres fronting Biscayne Bay, waterway off Bay, 15 min. to Miami Int'l. Airport. 3-bdr. (plus 1 staff room; staff suite) Bermuda-style residence, in superb cond., cabana, boat house, garage, orchid house; pool, tennis court, dock. *Local Agent: Esslinger-Wooten-Maxwell, Inc.*, Realtors 1553 San Ignacio Ave., Coral Gables 33146, tel. 305/667-8871.

Palm Beach Classic
Palm Beach, Florida Sold
205-ft. frontage on Lake Worth; 10,500 sq. ft. single-level contemporary w/3 bdrs., 5½ bths., serv. qtrs. Marble dance floor adjacent to heated pool; cabana w/2 bths., liv., din., kit; yacht-capacity dock. *Sotheby Parke Bernet International Realty Corp.*, Brokers, 155 Worth Ave., Palm Beach 33480, tel. 305/659-3555.

Saddle Cay
Exuma Cays, The Bahamas $500,000
30-min. flight S.E. of Nassau, private 90-acre island 59–80 ft. above sea level. Numerous beaches, all watersports. 3 small concrete & rock houses, cottage. *Local Agent: Chester Thompson Real Estate*, P.O. Box 1688, Nassau, Bahamas, tel. 809/322-4777.

Elegant John's Island Residence
John's Island, Florida Sold
1 hr. N. of Palm Beach, 2 hrs. from Miami, 5-bdr./5-bth. 1975 Georgian-style residence, in excel. cond. Floor-to-ceiling windows, French doors, garden off master suite; octagonal cabana w/bar, bath; pool. *Local Agent: John's Island*, John's Island Drive, Vero Beach, Fla. 32960, tel. 305/231-0900.

Mediterranean Villa
Palm Beach, Florida Sold
El Vedado Way, a few steps from ocean & Lake Worth. 18-room Spanish/Mediterranean-style residence built around interior courtyard; pool, 5 bdrs., 5 bths., staff apt., central heat, a/c. *Sotheby Parke Bernet International Realty Corp.*, Brokers, 155 Worth Ave., Palm Beach 33480, tel. 305/659-3555.

Regency Villa
Palm Beach, Florida Sold
Parc Monceau, 75-ft. frontage on Lake Worth, 4-bdr./4½-bth. Regency-style house w/loggia opening from salon onto pool terrace over lake. 2 garages. Offered w/adjoining larger lot to south; all frontage bulkheaded. *Sotheby Parke Bernet International Realty Corp.*, Brokers, 155 Worth Ave., Palm Beach 33480, tel. 305/659-3555.

Waterside Residence
Boca Raton, Florida Sold
On grounds of Royal Palm Yacht & C.C., 40 mi. N. of Miami, 7-bdr./7-bth. residence w/staff room, cabana, darkroom. 288 ft. frontage on waterway. Security, fire, intercom systems throughout. *Local Agent: Ronan Realty*, 95 East Palmetto Park Road, Boca Raton 33432, tel. 305/395-0000.

Unicorn Cay
Eleuthera, Bahamas Sold
1½ mi. S. of Governor's Harbor, 415 acres w/3,675-ft. Atlantic Beachfront. U-Shaped 4-bdr./4-bth. single-story residence ideal for clubhouse; w/ all rooms opening to central 50′ × 50′ courtyard. Ample grounds for golf course w/ inland lake, near Windermere Island Club. *Sotheby Parke Bernet International Realty Corp.*, Brokers, 155 Worth Ave., Palm Beach, Fla. 33480, tel. 305/659-3555.

Caribbean Retreat
Windermere Island, Bahamas $950,000
E. of Eleuthera, 82 unimproved beachfront acres on northern tip of Windermere w/road access; boat house. 6,000 ft. waterfrontage on Atlantic & Savannah Sound. Ideal development for several villa homesites. *Local Agent: Belmont Real Estate, Ltd.*, Governor's Harbour, Eleuthera, tel. 809/332-2301.

Oaklawn Manor
Franklin, Louisiana Sold
2 hrs. W. of New Orleans, 2,890 ft. on Bayou Teche, beaut. maintained antebellum plantation. 75 acres w/formal gardens, olympic pool. 1837 neo-Classical 6-bdr. house, 9 fireplaces, 14-ft. ceils., great hall. Cabana; aviary; guesthouse; barn. *Local Agent: Farnsworth - Samuel, Ltd.* 300 Board of Trade Place, New Orleans, 70130, tel. 504/525-4211.

Ibis Island Apartment
Palm Beach, Florida Sold
On the Intracoastal Waterway, Tower of Vallencay condo. apt. house, w/pool, sauna, excel. security, 5-room penthouse w/100-ft. terrace, air & intracoastal views. In *Architectural Digest*. Furnished or unfurnished. *Sotheby Parke Bernet International Realty Corp.*, Brokers, 155 Worth Ave., Palm Beach 33480, tel. 305/659-3555.

St. Charles Avenue Residence
New Orleans, Louisiana   *Sold*
St. Charles Ave. at State St., stone & brick 10-room French 18th C.-style 1968 residence. 4 bdrs., each w/ onyx bth. Built-in stereo, t.v.; central a/c; elev. & dumbwaiter. Pool. *Local Agent: Farnsworth-Samuel Ltd.*, 1521 Washington Ave., New Orleans, 70115, tel. 504/891-6400.

Dumaine Street Townhouse
New Orleans, Louisiana   *Sold*
In French Quarter, 2½-story 1830's brick townhouse, fully renov. in '70-s w/ 5 apts., each w/ separate access. Elev., sprinkler; 3-car carriageway. *Local Agent: Farnsworth-Samuel, Ltd.*, 300 Board of Trade Pl., New Orleans 70130, tel. 504/525-4211.

WEST

Central Texas Estate
Bryan, Texas $785,000
Brazos County, 90 mi. from Houston, 7.57 heavily wooded acres w/St. Augustine lawns, pool pavilion, putting green, 5-bdr./4-bth. Greek Revival-style house, in excel. cond. Fine chandeliers, wallcoverings, mantels, statuary. *Local Agent: John Daugherty, Inc.*, Realtors, 550 South Post Oak Rd., Houston 77056, tel. 713/626-3930.

River Oaks Residence
Houston, Texas   *Sold*
5 mi. W. of business district, 1½ fenced wooded acres. 2-story contemp. built in '61, renov. in '73 & '76, w/ central heat, a/c, underground sprinkler, outside lighting. 4 bdrs., 4 bths., staff room w/ bth. Formal interiors w/ fine moldings, marble floors, expanses of glass. *Local Agent: John Daugherty, Inc.*, Realtors, 550 South Post Oak Rd., Houston 77056, tel. 713/626-3930.

"Madewood"
Houston, Texas   *Sold*
Sherwood Forest, Memorial District, 1.3 wooded acres w/ badminton court, heated pool, garden patios. 5-bdr./5½-bth. plantation colonial-style residence built in '63. Gazebo, game house/grill. Near Houston & River Oaks C.C.'s. *Local Agent: John Daugherty, Inc.*, Realtors, 550 South Post Oak Rd., Houston 77056, tel. 713/626-3930.

Jack Rabbit Hill
Kerrville, Texas $550,000
Rivehill Estates section on Guadalupe River, 75 mi. to San Antonio, 90 mi. to Austin. 1½ beaut. landscaped acres w/ 5-bdr. 5½-bth. brick residence w/ terraces, balconies, patio gardens, pool. Guest house; garage. *Local Agent: John Daugherty, Inc.*, Realtors, 550 South Post Oak Rd., Houston 77056, tel. 713/626-3930.

#18 Courtlandt Place
Houston, Texas   *Sold*
5 min. from downtown, restricted residential block, 3-story Spanish/Prairie-style house c. 1910, renov. in '75, in superb cond. w/ fine orig. details. 5 bdrs., 5½ bths. Central heat, a/c; elev. Garage w/ serv. qtrs., guest house; pool. *Local Agent: John Daugherty, Inc.*, Realtors, 550 South Post Oak Rd., Houston 77056, tel. 713/626-3930.

"Treetops"
Houston, Texas $885,000
River Oaks, 15 min. to downtown, 1968 brick & glass contemp. built around tree-filled atrium, courtyards. 3 bdrs., 4 bths., staff bdr. Elev. to liv. room, lounge, "disco" upstairs. Guest house; pool; 2 garages. Burglar & fire alarms. *Local Agent: John Daugherty, Inc.*, Realtors, 550 South Post Oak Rd., Houston 77056, tel. 713/626-3930.

Memorial Contemporary
Houston, Texas   *Sold*
Farnham Park, 2½ wooded acres overlooking Buffalo Bayou w/ tropical pool, waterfall. 4-bdr./5½-bth. luxurious brick & glass contemp. Built-in TV, stereo, movie screen; burglar & fire alarms. Pool house. 24-hr. guard house in Farnham Park. *Local Agent: John Daugherty, Inc.*, Realtors, 550 South Post Oak Rd., Houston 77056, tel. 713/626-3930.

The Curtis Mansion
Belton, Texas $295,000
1 hr. to Austin, 3 hrs. to Houston, 1902/04 Edwardian landmark residence, carefully preserved, renov. in '74 w/ 4 income-prod. suites, each w/ bdr., bth., kit., liv. room. 9 fireplaces, stained glass, oak paneling. 2-bdr. apt. in garage. *Local Agent: John Daugherty, Inc.*, Realtors, 550 South Post Oak Rd., Houston 77056, tel. 713/626-3930.

"Cielo" *Dallas, Texas* $1,500,000
5 mi. S. of Denton, 12 mi. to Dallas/Ft. Worth Airport, 83.7 acres w/ 7,800-ft. frontage on Lake Dallas. 4-bdr. residence; 3-bdr. bunkhouse; theatre bldg., sound stage, movie set. Pool, tennis court, golf course. Heliport, grass landing strip. *Local Agent: Erle Rawlins, Jr.*, Realtors, 6725 Snider Plaza, Dallas 75205, tel. 214/363-1555.

Five Angels Ranch $900,000
Sonoita, Arizona   *(furnished)*
Elgin, Santa Cruz County, 64 mi. from Tucson, 7,150 fenced acres (150 deeded, 7,000 perpetual lease) in wet valley surrounded by Huachuca, Patagonia, Santa Rita & Whetstone Mts. 5-bdr./4½-bth. contemp. white-wash stucco & concrete residence; mgr.'s house, barns, corrals. Livestock, equipt. incl. *Local Agent: Bidegain Realty, Inc.*, P.O. box 17930, Tucson, Ariz. 85731, tel. 602/298-1855.

Desert Resort Estate $1,600,000
Palm Springs, California (partially furnished)
Thunderbird Heights, finest desert resort area in U.S.; 2½ acres w/ luxurious stone, glass, marble single-level contemp. (in *Architectural Digest*) 2-bdr. guest house; tennis pavilion, pool w/ waterfall, outdoor marble dance floor. Gated & guarded grounds. *Local Agent: Mimi Styne & Associates*, Realtors, 9606 Santa Monica Blvd., Beverly Hills, Cal. 90210, tel. 213/273-4111.

Montecito Contemporary
Santa Barbara, California   *Sold*
6 acres overlooking Birnam Wood C.C. & Pacific coast w/ citrus orchards, avocado trees. 1972–74 poured concrete & glass contemp. w/ 2 bdrs; 2-bdr. guest house; pool; garage. Intercom, a/c, built-in stereo, air purification, outside lighting, sprinkler systems. *Local Agent: Mimi Styne & Associates*, Realtors, 9606 Santa Monica Blvd., Beverly Hills, Cal., 90210, tel. 213/273-4111.

PHOTOGRAPHERS

Gil Amiaga: 11–12, 25–45, 54–55, 59–61, 82
Jaime Ardiles–Arce: 47 (pool)
Champion Pictures: 104
Margaret Cohn: 63
Max Eckert: 120–121
Rick Gardner: 108–117
Horst: 107, 118–119
N. Jane Iseley: 20, 64–81, 84–88, 90–93, 96–98, 99 (Waterside Residence)
Mort Kaye: 99 (Regency Villa)
Nathaniel Lieberman: 24, 52–53
Frank Lotz Miller: 102–103
Fred Packard: 89
Louis Reens: 46–47
Paul Rico: 106
Ezra Stoller: 94
Stanley Toogood: 83, 95, 100–101
Bill Van Calsem: 105
Bob Wands: 16–17